SELF-ESTEEM, SELF-IMAGE, SELF-WORTH

OVERCOMING FEELINGS OF BEING "LESS THAN"

Table of Contents

- Many of us carry around feelings of being and feeling "Less Than" others all of our adult lives. Perhaps we haven't shed childhood or teenage struggles of comparing ourselves to other who are better, prettier, sexier, more popular, smarter, more capable and far more successful than us. This battle of insufficiency or inferiority is the boogey man that keeps us from becoming our best selves. This min—course teaches us how to build, honor, and grow our own sense of self-worth, - esteem, and -image to become far better adjusted to life and others in our minds and in reality. We are always good enough and worth it, so give yourself permission to overcome what has long held you back from being your very best self!

21-DAY HAPPINESS
WORKOUT & KICKSTART
M. Fenton Deutsch
REVOLUTIONARY, NEW WAY
TO BEAT THE BLUES
& TRANSFORM YOUR LIFE
HAPPINESS
HEROES
FREEDOM
REVOLUTION

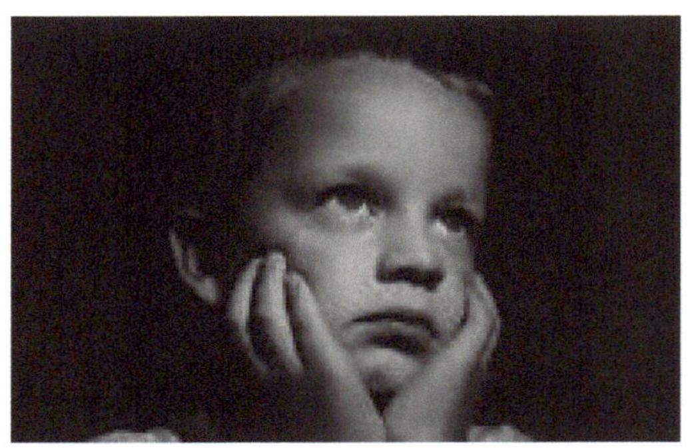

Mitch Before @ Age 55

Mitch After @ Age 62

- 310 lbs.
- *On 15 Medications
- Walking with a cane
- Workaholic
- Addicted to Alcohol & Pills
- Kids & ex-wife hate me
- Few Friends
- Angry & Burnt Out
- Lonely, Irritable, Discontent
- Couch Potato
- Very Sad & Mad

- 199 lbs.
- *Medication Free
- *Workout 5 days/week – totally buff
- Doing what I love with total balance
- Substance Free
- Healed relationships with Family & Friends
- Deep & Loving Friendships at home and at work.
- Free from my past and living in the incredible flow and gifts of my life.
- Meditate & do Yoga, Spin & Cross Fit
- Happy, fulfilled & smiling, relaxed & truly grateful to be alive! At peace with my life & the universe

- We're always comparing ourselves to other people & falsely believe we never "measure up"

- We never feel good enough, good looking enough, thin enough, confident enough, important enough, worthy of others' love, attention, praise

- Others are always better, smarter, sexier, more successful than us

- This pisses us off and makes us sad

- We accumulate and hold onto negative feelings like shame, resentment, anger, fear, remorse, self-pity

- We often turn these feelings inward or act out with others; We do harmful things to drown our feelings

- We find these negative feelings and attitudes uncomfortable, but prefer to hang on to them out of fear rather than face or deal with them

- These negative feelings/beliefs are irrational and most often not true

- Feelings aren't necessarily facts – but they CAN be appear to be the "boogeyman"

- These feelings and false beliefs lie to us telling us that we're never good enough – just not enough

- This keeps us from changing in positive ways; Keeps us from growing as human beings

- We pay a terrible price and teach others to do the same

- We remain stuck in this illusion of comparative failure and inferiority

- We lose what is already ours – confidence, peace-of-mind, knowing that we are just as good as anyone else and have nothing to prove

- Lack of validation as a child that we were enough

- Traumatic experience as a child or teenager – abuse, bullying, humiliation, harassment, social awkwardness

- Distortion and misinformation from social media -- FOMO

- Lack of praise and love from parents, adults, loved ones, friends

- Irrational fear, inability to challenge irrational thoughts and attitudes

- Self-Incrimination and being oh so hard on ourselves – more so than others

- Negative self-talk

- Fear of what might happen of we turn out to be good enough or even better

- Poor life processing skills, poor communication and relationship skills

- Immature emotional intelligence

- Come to know it's an utter lie – Nobody but us believes that we are inferior in any way

- Understand these feelings are not facts, but we come to think they are 100% real and true

- Learn these false feelings and beliefs are a choice and we choose out of fear and false illusion. The terrible result is that we become the inferior person that we think we are – it's a self-fulfilling prophecy

- Gather the strength to challenge this dis-ease and prove ourselves wrong

- Come to believe you can – or at least believe that I believe for now

- Become the person that we most feared – successful, self-confident, knowing that we're always good enough, pretty enough, sexy enough, smart enough, deserving and capable enough

- Stop comparing ourselves to others – only to ourselves. Other people are none of our business

- Go inside and replace broken skills and strategies with good ones

- Surround ourselves with positive, loving, and compassionate people who will support our choice and journey to change into the person we were always meant to be!

Self-confidence is linked to almost every element involved in a happy life (Psychology Today Barbara Markway Ph.D, author of Shyness is Nice):

- Less Fear and Anxiety

- Greater Motivation

- More Resilience

- Improved Relationships

- Stronger Sense of Your Authentic Self

- like and value yourself as a person.

- are able to make decisions and assert yourself.

- recognize your strengths and positives.

- feel able to try new or difficult things.

- show kindness towards yourself.

- move past mistakes without blaming yourself unfairly.

- take the time you need for yourself.

- People with healthy self-esteem feel confident in their own opinions, interests, and beliefs. … They look for reasons to release others and believe in the ability of others to make decisions. People who have healthy self-esteem themselves are better able to respect and appreciate the abilities and skills of others.

- People with a strong sense of self-worth exhibit a number of characteristics. When you see these characteristics reflected in yourself and your actions, you'll know you've arrived: They appreciate themselves and other people. They enjoy growing as a person and finding fulfillment and meaning in their lives.

- People who have high self-esteem have confidence in their own abilities. They believe in themselves. They recognize what they're good at, are confident that they are able to improve where necessary and unlike people with low self-esteem, believe that they deserve to do better.

10 CHARACTERISTICS OF PEOPLE WITH HIGH SELF-ESTEEM

- By S. Renee Smith, Vivian Harte author of Self-Esteem For Dummies

- People with a strong sense of self-worth exhibit a number of characteristics. When you see these characteristics reflected in yourself and your actions, you'll know you've arrived:

- They appreciate themselves and other people.

- They enjoy growing as a person and finding fulfillment and meaning in their lives.

- They are able to dig deep within themselves and be creative.

- They make their own decisions and conform to what others tell them to be and do only when they agree.

- They see the world in realistic terms, accepting other people the way they are, while pushing themselves to change in a more positive and confident direction.

- They can easily concentrate on solving problems in their lives.

- Their relationships are loving and respectful.

- They have thought about what their values are, identified them, and live according to these values every day.

- They speak up, calmly and kindly telling others their opinions and what their own wants and needs are.

- They endeavor to make a constructive difference in other people's lives.

WHAT IS SELF-WORTH?

- Self worth is the opinion you have about yourself and the value you place on yourself. An example of self worth is your belief that you are a good person who deserves good things or your belief that you are a bad person who deserves bad things.

- Self-esteem refers to a person's beliefs about their own worth and value. It also has to do with the feelings people experience that follow from their sense of worthiness or unworthiness. Self-esteem is important because it heavily influences people's choices and decisions.

- Confidence is a feeling of trust in someone or something. To be self-confident is to have confidence in yourself. Self-confident people don't doubt themselves. This is usually a positive word: you can be self-confident without being cocky, arrogant, or overconfident.

- Everyone knows that self-confidence is very important but what is not known to everyone is the degree of its importance. ... Self confidence can change your whole life to the better while lack of confidence will definitely have a negative effect on your social relations, career, achievements and even your mood.

- Your self-image is a mental picture of yourself, both as a physical body and an individual. When you think about yourself, the feelings and images that come up are important. A healthy body image means that you see yourself as you really are and that you feel good in your own skin.

- Self-image is important because how we think about ourselves affects how we feel about ourselves and how we interact with others and the world around us. A positiveself-image can boost our physical, mental, social, emotional, and spiritual well-being.

- Low self-esteem is characterized by a lack of confidence and feeling badly about oneself. People with low self-esteem often feel unlovable, awkward, or incompetent. … "As observers of our own behavior, thoughts, and feelings, we not only register these phenomena in consciousness but also pass judgement on them.

- Some of the many causes of low self-esteem may include: Unhappy childhood where parents (or other significant people such as teachers) were extremely critical. Poor academic performance in school resulting in a lack of confidence. Ongoing stressful life event such as relationship breakdown or financial trouble.

- Social withdrawal.

- Anxiety and emotional turmoil.

- Lack of social skills and self confidence. ...

- Less social conformity.

- Eating disorders.

- Inability to accept compliments.

- An Inability to see yourself 'squarely' - to be fair to yourself.

- Accentuating the negative.

- People with low self-esteem are more troubled by failure and tend to exaggerate events as being negative. For example, they often interpret non critical comments as critical. They are more likely to experience social anxiety and low levels of interpersonal confidence.

- Low self-esteem is characterized by a lack of confidence and feeling badly about oneself. People with low self-esteem often feel unlovable, awkward, or incompetent. … Often, individuals lacking self-esteem see rejection and disapproval even when there isn't any.

- Shame. Shame is one of the main symptoms of low self-esteem. ...

- Pessimism. Feelings of pessimism are a good indication that self-esteem may be suffering. ...

- Exaggeration. ...

- Blame. ...

- Lack of Boundaries. ...

- Putting Others Down. ...

- Social Withdrawal. ...

- Physical Symptoms.

- Which of the contributing factors described in this section resonate the most with you?

- What specific experiences in your life do you think had the biggest negative effects on your self-confidence?

TAKE A SELF-CONFIDENCE QUIZ

- Take this self-confidence quiz developed by Barbara Markway Ph.D. from Psychology Today:

- Self-confidence begins with knowing yourself. You might also enjoy spending some time answering these questions designed to help increase your confidence level: https://www.psychologytoday.com/us/blog/shyness-is-nice/201810/how-confident-are-you-really

- Rating yourself A, B, or C (with A being the strongest and C the least): I have a realistic sense of my strengths and weaknesses. I am willing to take risks for something I believe in. I take time to remember my past successes. I recognize failure as a part of life. I can cope with unexpected changes. I am comfortable asking for help and support. I know what I value in life. My actions generally line up with my values. I don't give up easily. I realize not everyone will like or approve of me. I have a sense of my inherent worth. I understand setbacks are normal and to be expected. I don't beat up on myself when I'm going through a rough time. My thoughts don't paralyze me when trying something new.

HOW DO YOU FIX LOW SELF-ESTEEM?

- like and value yourself as a person.

- are able to make decisions and assert yourself.

- recognise your strengths and positives.

- feel able to try new or difficult things.

- show kindness towards yourself.

- move past mistakes without blaming yourself unfairly.

- take the time you need for yourself.

HOW TO DEVELOP SELF-CONFIDENCE

"Low self-esteem is like driving through life with your hand brake on." -- Maxwell Maltz

- 10 Things You Can Do to Boost Self-Confidence:

- 1. Visualize yourself as you want to be. 2. Affirm yourself. 3. Do one thing that scares you every day. 4. Question your inner critic. 5. Take the 100 days of rejection challenge. 5. Take the 100 days of rejection challenge. 6. Set yourself up to win. 7. Help someone else. 8. Care for yourself. 9. Create personal boundaries. 10. Shift to an equality mentality.

- https://www.entrepreneur.com/article/281874

- https://www.wikihow.com/Build-Self-Confidence

- https://www.youtube.com/watch?v=L-F3ts7Fu10

- https://www.youtube.com/watch?v=20p5o6QaQfg

- https://www.youtube.com/watch?v=XNVHeW-TPPc

- In order to build a healthy sense of confidence, we need to stop comparing ourselves to others. Instead of worrying about how you measure up to the people around you, think about the type of person you want to be. Set goals and take actions that are consistent with your own values.

- Looking to boost your confidence by measuring yourself against others is a big mistake. Dr. Kristen Neff explains, "Our competitive culture tells us we need to be special and above average to feel good about ourselves, but we can't all be above average at the same time...There is always someone richer, more attractive, or successful than we are." When we evaluate ourselves based on external achievements, other people's perceptions and competitions, "our sense of self-worth bounces around like a ping-pong ball, rising and falling in lock-step with our latest success or failure." Social media only exacerbates this problem, as people post their picture-perfect moments and shiny achievements, which we compare to our tarnished, flawed everyday lives.

- Self-confidence and self-esteem are built on self-RESPECT. If you live a life that is in line with your own principles, whatever they may be, you are more likely to respect yourself, feel more confident, and even do better in life. For example, a study at the University of Michigan found that students "who based their self-esteem on internal sources—such as being a virtuous person or adhering to moral standards—were found to receive higher grades and less likely to use alcohol and drugs or to develop eating disorders."

- To feel good about yourself, it is important to have integrity and make sure that your actions match your words. For example, if eating healthy and looking your best are important values to you, you will feel better if you maintain a healthy lifestyle. When your actions don't match your words, you are far more vulnerable to self-attacks. The inner critic loves to point out these shortcomings. It is valuable to think about your core principles and act in line with those beliefs when you are trying to boost your confidence.

- As human beings, we tend to feel good about ourselves when we do something meaningful, taking part in activities that are larger than ourselves and/or helpful to others. This is a beautiful way to go about building confidence and developing healthier levels of self-esteem.

- Studies show that volunteering has a positive effect on how people feel about themselves. Researcher Jennifer Crocker suggests that you find "a goal that is bigger than the self." When pursuing meaningful activities, it is important to think about what feels the most significant to you. For some people, this may mean volunteering at a homeless shelter, tutoring children, taking part in local politics, gardening with friends, etc. Follow the breadcrumbs of where you find meaning, and you may find your self-esteem along the way.

- Once we believe in ourselves, we can risk curiosity, wonder, spontaneous delight, or any experience that reveals the human spirit. – E.E. Cummings

- 1.. Groom yourself 2. Dress nicely 3. Photoshop your self-image 4. Think positive 5. Kill negative thoughts 6. Get to know yourself. 7. Act positive 8. Be kind and generous. 9. Get prepared 10. Know your principles and live them. 11. Speak slowly 12. Stand tall. 13. Increase competence 14. Set a small goal and achieve it 15. Change a small habit. 16. Focus on solutions. 17. Smile 18. Volunteer. 19. Be grateful. 20. Exercise 21. Empower yourself with knowledge 22. Do something you've been procrastinating on. 23. Get active. 24. Work on small things. 25. Clear your desk.

- More Good Stuff To Do: Get Off Social Media. Learn to Meditate, Practice Mindfulness, Unstress – Focus on the Now – Living in the Present Moment, Learn to Have Fun, Have Memorable Experience, Spend Time Helping Others, Volunteering, Work on Building Great Relationships, Do Esteem-able Things!!

- Somehow I can't believe that there are any heights that can't be scaled by a man who knows the secrets of making dreams come true. This special secret, it seems to me, can be summarized in four C s. They are curiosity, confidence, courage, and constancy, and the greatest of all is confidence. When you believe in a thing, believe in it all the way, implicitly and unquestionable. – Walt Disney

- "You yourself, as much as anybody in the entire universe, deserve your love and affection"– Buddha

- "Until you value yourself, you won't value your time. Until you value your time, you will not do anything with it."– M. Scott Peck

- "Confront the dark parts of yourself, and work to banish them with illumination and forgiveness. Your willingness to wrestle with your demons will cause your angels to sing." August Wilson

- "Never be bullied into silence. Never allow yourself to be made a victim. Accept no one's definition of your life, but define yourself." Harvey Fierstein

- "Wanting to be someone else is a waste of the person you are." Marilyn Monroe

- "I'm Dylan. I'm so cool. I want to date myself, but I don't know how! You want to date me instead? You're so lucky!" Rick Riordan, The Lost Hero

- "That's what real love amounts to - letting a person be what he really is. Most people love you for who you pretend to be. To keep their love, you keep pretending - performing. You get to love your pretence. It's true, we're locked in an image, an act - and the sad thing is, people get so used to their image, they grow attached to their masks. They love their chains. They forget all about who they really are. And if you try to remind them, they hate you for it, they feel like you're trying to steal their most precious possession." — Jim Morrison

- "One's dignity may be assaulted, vandalized and cruelly mocked, but it can never be taken away unless it is surrendered." — Michael J. Fox

- love yourself to get anything done in this world."– Lucille Ball

- https://www.ted.com/search?q=self-esteem

- https://www.ted.com/talks/meaghan_ramsey_why_thinking_you_re_ugly_is_bad_for_you

- https://www.ted.com/talks/carol_dweck_the_power_of_believing_that_you_can_improve?referrer=playlist-talks_for_when_you_feel_like_y

- https://www.ted.com/talks/mindy_scheier_how_adaptive_clothing_empowers_people_with_disabilities

- https://www.ted.com/talks/amy_adkins_3_tips_to_boost_your_confidence

- https://www.ted.com/speakers/guy_winch

- https://www.ted.com/talks/guy_winch_the_case_for_emotional_hygiene?referrer=playlist-talks_for_when_you_feel_like_y

For Kids:

- https://www.youtube.com/watch?v=ySNrWiq9zk8

- https://www.youtube.com/watch?v=aneMtTfe0CA

- https://www.youtube.com/watch?v=j2oCP_wk1TA

- https://www.youtube.com/watch?v=wC9S_fFMnaU

For Teens:

- https://www.youtube.com/watch?v=BZ05M1UhPrY

- https://www.youtube.com/watch?v=CxsBxhwzw58

- https://www.youtube.com/watch?v=1iINhdvyAbI

- https://www.youtube.com/watch?v=_zO4JnWrLBU

- Many of us struggle with feeling less than

- We experience poor self-esteem, sense of self-, poor self-worth, lack of confidence

- It's the boogeyman

- Practice self-confidence tools

- If you don't believe you're good enough, nobody else will

- You have the power to change the way you feel

- You must take responsibility for all of you – good and bad

- You are not a victim, but can become a power of example for others to take charge of their lives

- It's a process, so give yourself a pat on the back today for starting on your journey to healing how you feel about yourself and break-free

- THE HEALING ACADEMY (url)/facebook group)
- Healing from Toxic Parents
- Happiness Mastery System
- 21-Day Happiness Challenge
- Making Love Work
- Making Life Work
- Spiritual Journey
- Mindfulness & Meditation
- All my e-books

www.ingramcontent.com/pod-product-compliance
Lightning Source LLC
Chambersburg PA
CBHW040051240726
48664CB00004B/1153